Love
from
Piglet

xx

To . . . .

With love from

. . . .

Love from

Piglet

xx

A.A. Milne

Illustrations by E.H. Shepard

EGMONT

Hand in hand we come
Christopher Robin and I
To lay this book in your lap.
Say you're surprised?
Say you like it?

♥

Say it's just what you wanted?
Because it's yours —
Because
we
love
you.

♥

Love
Letters

Words of Love

They began to talk in a friendly way
about this and that, and Piglet said,
'If you see what I mean, Pooh,'
and Pooh said, 'It's just
what I think myself, Piglet...'

Love
Delights
in Praise

Piglet said that he thought it
was a Cunning Trap.
Pooh was very proud
when he heard this.

♥

Love
Casteth
Out Fear

Piglet wasn't afraid if
he had Christopher Robin
with him, so off they went...

Love
Token

'I'll give him a balloon. I've got
one left from my party.'
'That, Piglet, is a *very* good idea.
It is just what Eeyore wants
to cheer him up.'

Missing You...

BANG!!!???***!!!
Piglet thought that he was
now alone in the moon or
somewhere, and would never see
Christopher Robin or Pooh
or Eeyore again.

Loving
and *Giving*

'Many happy returns of the day,'
said Piglet.
'Meaning me?'
'Of course, Eeyore.'
'My birthday?'
'Yes.'

'Me having a real birthday?'
'Yes, Eeyore, and I've
brought you a present.'

Gifts
of
Love

'I'm very glad,' said Piglet
happily, 'that I thought of
giving you Something to
put in a Useful Pot.'

Baby Love

'Are you all right, Roo, dear?'
said Kanga.
Piglet made a squeaky
Roo-noise from the bottom
of Kanga's pocket.

Quality
Time

Every Tuesday Piglet spent
the day with his great friend
Christopher Robin.
... So they were all
happy again.

Loving
Company

'If only I had been in Pooh's
house, or Christopher Robin's
house, or Rabbit's house when
it began to rain, then I should
have had Company all this time,
instead of being here all alone...'

Love
Song I

So Pooh hummed it to him, all
the seven verses, and Piglet said
nothing, but just stood and
glowed. For never before had
anyone sung ho for Piglet
(*Piglet*) ho all by himself.

Sharing

It would have been jolly to talk...
it wasn't much good having
anything exciting like floods,
if you couldn't share them
with somebody.

♥

Love
and
Friendship

And then he gave a very long
sigh and said, 'I wish Pooh
were here. It's so much
more friendly with two.'

Love

Conquers All

You can imagine Piglet's joy
when at last the ship
came in sight
of him.

The good ship
Brain of Pooh

(*Captain*, C. Robin; *1st Mate*, P. Bear)

Help Those You Love

'*You* have a house, Piglet, and I
have a house... but poor Eeyore
has nothing. So what I've been
thinking is: Let's build
him a house.'

'That,' said Piglet, 'is a Grand
Idea. Where shall we build it?'

Affection...

Pooh and Piglet
came up and hugged
Christopher Robin...

. . . and
Comfort

'I can hear it, can't you?' said
Piglet, anxiously, as they got near.
'There!' he said. 'Isn't it *awful*?'
Piglet held on tight to
Christopher Robin's hand.

Loving
is Forgiving

'You fell on me,' said Piglet.
'I didn't mean to,' said
Pooh, sorrowfully.
'But I'm all right now, Pooh,
and I *am* so glad it was you.'

Words of Love and Praise

'Christopher Robin, I've found
Small!' cried Piglet.
'Well done, Piglet,' said
Christopher Robin. And at
these encouraging words Piglet
felt quite happy again...

♥

Love
Song II

I could spend a happy morning
Seeing Piglet.
And I couldn't spend
a happy morning
Not seeing Piglet.

Brotherly
Love

Piglet took Pooh's arm, in case
Pooh was frightened.
'Is it One of the Fiercer Animals?'
he said, looking the other way.

Flowers of Love I

It suddenly came over him that
nobody had ever picked Eeyore a
bunch of violets... he thought how
sad it was to be an Animal who
had never had a bunch of violets
picked for him...

II

So he hurried out again, saying
'Eeyore, Violets' and 'Violets,
Eeyore,' in case he forgot, because
it was that sort of a day, and he
picked a large bunch and
trotted along, smelling them,
and feeling very happy...

Loving
Concern

'Well, if we all threw stones and
things into the river on one side
of Eeyore, the stones would make
waves, and the waves would
him to the other side.'

'Suppose we hit
him by mistake?'
said Piglet anxiously.

Love-All

'Tigger is all right, *really*,'
said Piglet lazily.
'Of course he is,' said
Christopher Robin.
'Everybody is *really*,'
said Pooh.

Love
is Thoughtful

'... he'll be a Sad Tigger, and
Melancholy Tigger, a Small and
Sorry Tigger...' said Rabbit.
'I should hate him to go *on* being
Sad,' said Piglet doubtfully.

All for Love

Piglet sidled up to Pooh from
behind.
'Pooh!' he whispered.
'Yes, Piglet?'
'Nothing,' said Piglet,
taking Pooh's paw.

'I just wanted to
be sure of you.'

True Love

'Just the house for Owl.
Don't you think so, little Piglet?'
And then Piglet did a Noble
Thing... 'Yes, it's just the house for
Owl,' he said grandly. 'I hope
he'll be very happy in it.'

And then he gulped twice,
because he had
been very happy
in it himself.

Loves Me,
Loves Me Not

The Piglet was sitting on the
groundat the door of his
house blowing happily at a
dandelion and wondering whether
it would be this year, next year,
sometime, or never.

♥

Loving
Thoughts

Later on, Pooh and Piglet
walked home thoughtfully
together in the golden evening,
and for a long time they
were silent.

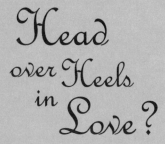

Head *over* Heels *in* Love?

Published in Great Britain 2002
by Egmont Books Limited
239 Kensington High Street
London W8 6SA

ISBN 1 4052 0443 5

3 5 7 9 10 8 6 4 2

Printed in Singapore

The
Wisdom
of
Pooh